T0131970

MIDDLETON
CORNER

By Wallace D. Campbell, Ph.D.

Forward by Joan Baxter, Greene County
Historical Society

Misty Morning at Middleton Corner - July 4, 2006

To order additional copies of this book, contact:
Xlibris
844-714-8691
www.Xlibris.com
Orders@Xlibris.com

ISBN: Softcover   978-1-4257-3517-3
         EBook   978-1-4771-6567-6

Library of Congress Control Number: 2006908706

Print information available on the last page

Rev. date: 12/02/2021

Table of Contents

Other Books Co-Authored With Grandsons

Did You Ever Wonder? An ABC Picture Book---------------------- © 2004 Xlibris

Who Taught Caterpillars to Spin Cocoons? ------------------------ © 2005 Xlibris

What Was God Thinking? An ABC Picture Book ------------------ © 2006 Xlibris

Dedication

This book is dedicated to John Middleton, Jr. who passed away a few days before his seventeenth birthday. He and his girlfriend, Karin Erd, left us when their lives were just beginning.

John Middleton, Jr.   1956-1973

You will not find it listed on a Greene County map, and if you don't look closely, you might just drive right past, but Middleton's Corner is there at the corner of US 68 and Spring Valley-Paintersville Road in Caesarscreek Township. There is no post office, no gas station and no school, although some years after Middleton's Corner was established, the Caesarscreek School opened not far away. The railroad did not come through the community to provide transportation of goods and services. In spite of the fact that it is not located on the Greene County map, or in any of the atlases, the State Highway Department feels that the community is important enough to have the name of the hamlet posted on the highway. When you near that corner, you will find a sign beside the road identifying the area as "Middleton Corner," then, in about two tenths of a mile, you will find another sign, facing the other direction with the same information.

The 1855 map of Greene County does not mention Middleton Corner, but it does list several Middleton families who lived in the vicinity. Although the highway sign designates the hamlet as Middleton Corner, most people call it Middleton's Corner. Then how did it ever get its name? It all began in 1825. After the Northwest Territory was opened for residents, settlers came into what would become Greene County to stake their claims and purchase land. When Ohio became a state in 1803, even more settlers thought it desirable to move here. People came from such places as Virginia and Kentucky when they heard of the rich farmland available for minimal amounts of money. Such was the case with brothers John and Thomas Middleton who were born in Berkley County, Virginia. They were interested in obtaining large parcels of land at reasonable prices which would be suitable for farming, thus they came to Ohio by horseback planning to purchase the land which they felt would be suitable.

After they made their purchase in 1825, they returned to their native Virginia where each of them got married. They persuaded their parents and other members of the family to come to the new state to make their homes as well. Their parents, Bethuel and Naomi Middleton, were as anxious as their sons to begin a new life here, and so the family finally arrived in Greene County with a six-horse team.

They had no trouble providing sheltering homes for their families, since the land was heavily timbered, and logs for houses were plentiful. Thomas had been engaged in the business of hauling by wagon train, and then later became a cattle buyer and pork packer. He bought and processed the pork in the area, then transported it to Cincinnati for sale. Several years later, his son, Lewis became a breeder of fine horses. His expertise in this endeavor provided many fine horses in this and adjacent counties. James married Angeline Musetter and, in time, her family also moved to Greene County.

James and his wife were the parents of ten children, all born at Middleton's Corner. Farming was the major industry in the community, which continued to grow, with more Middleton children continuing to live in the area. The 1855 Atlas of Greene County shows T. Middleton, J. Middleton, B. Middleton, and C. Middleton living in the vicinity of what was known even then as Middleton's Corner. The atlas also shows that there was some industry in the hamlet at one time. A blacksmith shop and a wagon shop were located there. By 1874, James, Thomas, G., and J were listed in the Greene County Atlas.

Farming and raising livestock were the main activities in which the family was engaged. Each generation improved the land and built new homes.

A general store was the main business in the hamlet for many years. Located on U. S. 68, it was easily accessible not only to those in the immediate neighborhood, but also to persons living nearby. It was originally owned by a family named Marshall who sold it to a Mr. Dowdell. Eventually Mr. Kirkpatrick bought the store, and employed two of the Middleton boys to work there. In 1958, brothers John and Robert Middleton, having worked for Mr. Kirkpatrick, bought the store. They kept the store open until 1973 when they sold the business. During their tenure, one could purchase groceries, fresh meat, fresh produce, gasoline, motor oil, kerosene and other necessities. You could also purchase a hand dipped ice cream cone for five cents a dip. The store building is still standing, but the five-cent a dip ice cream cones are no longer available. Tiffany Matthews owns the business now, which has children's toys, books, and other items for sale. The store is still easily accessible from the highway.

The tradition continues with the Middleton family and Middleton's Corner. John Middleton has lived at Middleton's Corner nearly all of his life, and continues to own property there. He and his wife are the only descendants of the original Middleton Family living in Middleton's Corner at the present time. Several houses, some new, some not so new, are now located on what was once land owned by the various members of the Middleton family.

John and Mona Faye Middleton

Matthew's Market

Gretchen Rives, *Xenia Daily Gazette* staff writer, wrote in an article published on September 5, 1984, in *The Gazette Midweek Section*, "Rural 'mom and pop' store lives on." When we moved to Middleton Corner in 1971 this was true. We were ten miles from the nearest town and right next door to us was a little country market where we could buy bread, milk and gasoline. As the commercial says, "It doesn't get much better than this!"

The Gravitt family started the store back in the 1930s and then the Marshall clan purchased it in the 1940s running it through the war years. I was born during that time in the spring of 1944. One of the things the Marshall family did was to collect used tires and batteries to support the war effort. In the 1950s the Boswell and Kirkpatrick families ran the store and this was followed by the Middleton, Shope and Alexander families through the 1970s.

John and Mona Faye Middleton ran the store when we moved to Middleton Corner in 1971. They sold the store to their son-in-law and daughter Joe and Cathy Shope. Our kids used to play with their kids through the fence that divided our properties.

The Shopes eventually sold the store to the Alexander family. Once Mrs. Alexander's mother accidentally locked herself in the basement of the store and we could hear her yelling for help from our house. My wife went to her rescue.

After the Alexanders, the owners were the Kylies, Connors, Gillems and eventually Phil and Sue Matthews. They changed the name to Matthew's Market. When Phil passed away, his daughter Tiffany took over the operation of the country market. Around this time new EPA regulations for underground gasoline tanks made it cost prohibitive to continue to sell gasoline at the market. This eventually led to its demise. Tiffany operated a Pizza Parlor from the site for a few years and has now converted it to a year-round flea market. It's sad to have lost the market, but we can still pick up a good bargain at Tiffany's

Bug Jar

When I was a sophomore at Greeneview High School, my science teacher, Ken Wilburn, required his students to make an insect collection. I think he required us to collect one hundred specimens. That may sound like a lot of insects, but farm boys know that at wheat harvest time all they have to do is climb in the back of a grain wagon and they can collect lots of different bugs. I'm not sure why but I remember the stinkbug as being one of the bugs you could count on finding in the wheat.

Now that I am a grandpa with five grandsons, one of my favorite activities is to take the boys out into the woods and yard and collect insects. No special equipment is required except a clear plastic jar. Grandma always has plenty of those setting in the cabinets just waiting to be used for such adventures.

There are many different varieties of insects at Middleton Corner. Tanner, one of the youngest of my grandsons, is particularly good at finding and catching bugs. If you could see into his jar, you would find a cicada, katydid, moth, assassin beetle, ladybug, bumblebee, and a Japanese beetle.

The Bug Jar is one of the most fun, fascinating and educational activities that I have been able to enjoy with my grandsons. If you ever hear me say that my grandsons bug me, you will really know what that means. It's a good thing!

Weavers' Convention

Heavy dew in the morning coupled with some creative weavers produces an art show of remarkable masterpieces. The display signals the end of summer and the coming of fall. Visitors to the weavers' convention can expect to get their feet wet and to walk into some silk strands suspended throughout the garden gallery. In this gallery, visitors are encouraged to take pictures. They must arrive early before the sun comes out and burns the fog away or they will not even be aware of the art show God provided that morning.

Naked Ladies Arrive at Middleton Corner

Although there is no convention center, campgrounds, or nudist colony, thousands of naked ladies converge on Middleton Corner every year the last week of July and the first week of August. They gather along the edge of the woods and stream. It is actually their second trip of the year. They arrived far less ostentatiously in early spring with the daffodils dressed in dark green. Like George Foreman's family, all the ladies bear the same name, *Lycoris squamigera*. They are more commonly known as surprise, magic, mystery, and resurrection lily or naked lady. Naked lady is my favorite term although my wife prefers that I refer to them as mystery lilies. I discovered it is better to follow her advice when looking for information about the lilies on a search engine, but it is a lot more fun to see the expressions on the faces of visitors to my garden when I tell them it is time for the naked ladies to arrive. In early spring the large bulbs send up dark green leaves slightly larger than daffodil leaves. However, unlike the daffodils, the naked ladies do not bloom at this time. This is the food making and storage stage of the plant. The leaves die toward the end of June, but something magical happens at the end of July and the first of August. A single naked stem mysteriously emerges from seemingly nowhere. In a few days a cluster of pink orchid flowers blossom at the top of the stem. Established massive beds of Naked Ladies are prolific bloomers (no pun intended). The plants can grow in the woods because their growth period occurs before the leaves come out on the trees and they can receive adequate sunlight for photosynthesis to occur. They are equally adapted to full sun locations. The bulbs can be dug, divided, and transplanted in either spring or summer.

Story Tellers

We have a story bench in the woods. It is one of the favorite places for two of my grandsons, Jacob and Isaac Wilkinson. We have authored many stories on this bench. In fact, we are working on our fourth book called, <u>The Story Bench</u>. It is a collection of stories that we have made up during their various visits to Middleton Corner.

Jacob and I co-authored <u>Did You Ever Wonder? An ABC Picture Book</u> when he was in preschool. Kyle Bryan, a Greeneview High School senior art student, illustrated the book.
Opposite pages have the same line using two different letters. For example, "Did you ever wonder who put the **(A a)** antlers on deer ….. and the **(B b)** bark in the dog?"

There was enough left over material from that book to write a second book called, <u>Who Taught Caterpillars to Spin Cocoons?</u> Jacob wanted to write the book for his younger brother, Isaac. Another GHS senior, Kim Spiller, illustrated the book for us. Opposing pages in this book emphasized similar actions such as "Who taught the cat to meow …. and the wolf to howl?" We added directions or questions to each page to encourage parents to interact with their children. On the two pages mentioned, the direction and question were "Point to the cat's whiskers and when do wolves howl?"

Finally, Isaac decided he wanted to write an ABC Picture Book just like his brother so we wrote <u>What Was God Thinking?</u> We wrote this book during a summer visit before he started kindergarten. GHS student, Shellie Carver, illustrated that book. The purpose of all three books is to help young children see God in all of creation. Once again the set up for the opposing pages in Isaac's book dealt with things from nature. For example, for **"G"** and **"H"** he said, "What was God thinking when He put the **g**low in the volcano …. and the **h**um in the **h**ummingbird?" The letter of the alphabet being emphasized was always colored red for easy identification.

Jacob has started writing chapter books on his own now, so maybe a famous author will come out of Middleton Corner.

Milkweed Jungle

Milkweed is a host plant for the monarch butterfly. The adult monarch lays her eggs on the plant and when the eggs hatch, the caterpillars feed on the leaves. A well chewed up plant is a good thing. It means you have a crop of monarch caterpillars feeding in your garden. With all the chemical sprays farmers use to control weeds in their fields, the milkweed is sometimes in short supply. When I noticed a milkweed sprout in my side yard a few years ago, I decided to stake it and let it grow in hopes of attracting more butterflies to my garden. It worked. I now have forty-three plants and the number keeps increasing every year.

I am amazed at the fragrance of the milkweed's pink flowers. When the milkweed blooms there are so many bees feeding on the nectar that you can actually hear the milkweed patch hum. The milkweeds grow tall when nurtured in a garden. I measured one of my plants at seven feet two inches.

Even the seedpods are fun on the milkweed plant. It puts out feathery, white parachutes that carry the seeds on the wind to far away places. Who knows? The milkweed plant growing in your garden may have come from a seed from the milkweed jungle at Middleton Corner.

Retired Caesarscreek Township Road Supervisor Jesse Wheelen stands in the milkweed patch. Jesse retired after twenty years maintaining the roads around Middleton Corner. I especially appreciated him on snowy mornings when I had to go to work. He always had the roads cleared except for the year of the big blizzard. That year, even the state highway crew had a snowplow stuck on Highway US 68 South.

Bird Poop Moth

We have a white vinyl gate in our backyard. You have to reach over the top to access the latch on the other side. This morning I noticed what I thought was bird poop on the top of the gate so I got a tissue to wipe it off. To my surprise, the bird poop flew away when I touched it! This piqued my interest so I got online or "Googled it" as my grandson says and typed in "bird poop moth." I didn't find much information about the moth, but I found lots of photos that other surprised nature enthusiasts had posted on the web. Mark Doerr of Cleveland, Ohio, noted with his picture of the moth, "I thought you might like another picture of the bird poop moth. I found this little guy sitting on the hood of my car one morning – looking exactly like bird poop." The moth is actually a Wood Nymph Moth in the genus Euthisanotia.

Another blogger asked if this was really a Bird Turd Moth. The answer he received was "Nah, but that is what it resembles. I would hazard a guess it is an example of protective coloration. It is also alliterative, which helps." I think he means that it rhymes.

Scientists theorize that this particular moth mimicry is a good thing because it allows the moth the opportunity to avoid being eaten by birds and survive to breed with other wood nymph moths. A bird is not likely to peck and taste its own feces.

Inelegant but effective, its dropping disguise is thought to discourage predators and help the larva survive long enough to metamorphose into a flight-ready moth.

Bird Poop Moth on mock orange bush

CHICKERY CHICK, CHA-LA, CHA-LA

I love it when the blue chicory blooms along the highway each summer. It brings back memories from my childhood and a silly children's song that I learned fifty plus years ago. When the chicory blooms, I always break out into a song even though I can't sing. My children endured it while they were growing up and now my grandchildren are the victims of my vocalizations. Funny thing though, it always makes them laugh. When I pick up young children to take them to church, they ask me to sing the "Banana" song when the chicory is in bloom. Santly-Joy, Inc., New York, copyrighted the song in 1945. Lyrics are by Sylvia Dee, and music by Sidney Lippman. The song goes like this:

> "Chickery Chick, Cha-la, Cha-la
> Chick-a-la Romey, In a Ba-nan-i-ka
> Bol-li-ka Wol-li-ka, Can't you see
> Chickery Chick is me."

The faster you try to sing the song, the sillier it becomes. Over time, I botched the last two lines changing it to "Follica, Wollika, can't you see? Chickery Chick it's me." I also changed Romey to Romeo.

Chicory grows in light and sandy soil making it an ideal plant for the gravel berm of a highway. It is a perennial that has a deep taproot that is almost impossible to pull out. It has tough, two to three foot high twig-like stems with bright blue flowers, resembling a coreopsis, arranged along the branching stems. I appreciate the highway crew, but I always hate it when the side of the highway is mowed while the chicory is blooming.

Moth Menagerie

Moths and butterflies have always fascinated me. I have been blessed with a summer phenomenon that has enabled me to see some of the most unique and colorful night flying moths in this area of Ohio. I have a nightlight attached to the end of the garage above the garage door. The moths are attracted to the light and come in great numbers during the night. In the morning I find a veritable cornucopia of different types and colors of moths on the garage door. They remain there until after the sun comes up and they fly away. Since I am an early riser, I am able to see these flying wonders. If I have the time and my camera I can capture their images to enjoy and share later. Some of my favorites are the Luna and Cecropia moths because of their size and color. I have already shared with you the story of the bird poop moth that is a novelty. There are several others that resemble dead leaves. Moths are masters of disguise. This is necessary because they have to conceal themselves somewhere during the day so birds, spiders, or other insect eaters do not eat them. I admire their fuzzy antennae and fuzzy feet.

The Passion of Middleton Corner

Passionflowers (*Passiflora* species) grow profusely at Middleton Corner. The mysterious vines emerge from the ground in late summer. I thought my vines had died since they had not come up in the spring like my other perennials. But once they emerge they grow quickly and twine around the fence where they are planted. They soon set an exotic bloom that is difficult to describe giving meaning to the cliché – a picture is worth a thousand words. The vines produce five inch, royal purple blooms with lacy corollas overlaying the petals. An ancient legend describing the religious symbolism of the passionflower helps with the description.

According to the legend, a 17th century Peruvian Jesuit priest discovered passionflowers. He had a vision that compared the various parts of the flower with the crucifixion. The ten faithful apostles present at the crucifixion were represented by the five petals and five sepals. Christ's wounds were represented by the five anthers. The pistils represented the nails, and the corona was His thorny crown. The leaves of the passion vine were Roman spears, and the tendrils were their whips.

The exotic blooms emit an intoxicating scent, and produce an edible fruit that has a flavor described as a combination of tropical pineapple and crisp white grapes. The rich nectar is a food source for adult butterflies. The leaves are an important food source for some of our most beautiful butterfly caterpillars, including the Gulf Fritillary and the Zebra Longwing. My son, Kevin, taught me about host plants for butterflies. Another example of a common host plant is the milkweed for monarch butterflies.

The passionflower is commonly called maypops, for the sound they make when stepped on. The leaves contain a natural sedative, and have been used as a remedy for nervousness and insomnia.

Sunrise, Sunset

There are many beautiful sunrises and sunsets at Middleton Corner. Sometimes part of the sunrise is hidden when the corn is as "high as an elephant's eye." I drive east on my way to work and I leave at sunrise giving me the opportunity to welcome many gorgeous mornings. On a recent morning, I could tell it was going to be a beautiful awakening of the day. The old adage "red in the morning, sailors take warning," does not apply to me. Red in the morning sky makes my heart beat faster because I know God is about to paint a masterpiece in the sky. On this particular day He overwhelmed me with His creativity. I travel the back roads to work so it is easy to stop and take pictures. As I approached the rise on Spring Valley Paintersville Road I had a spectacular view of the sunrise, but my camera was in my briefcase in the back seat and I missed the shot. I passed through Paintersville and stopped at the intersection with Hussey Pike. I jumped out of the car, opened the backdoor and retrieved my camera. I took a few pictures out of the passenger side window. I usually don't go down Hollingsworth Road, but I turned right this morning so I could see the sunrise out the driver's side window. I got some good pictures on the short trip down Hollingsworth to Mt. Carmel Road. This required a left turn and the sunrise was on my right again. This took me past farms and cornfields. The corn is high and tasseled in August, so I missed some of the changes. I was able to get a break in the corn and trees to capture the big round red ball as it broke the horizon. The cool breeze in my face, the refreshing morning air, and the beauty of the sunrise made me think of the song in Fiddler on the Roof.

"Sunrise, Sunset
Sunrise, Sunset
Swiftly flow the days.
Seedlings turn over night to sunflowers
blossoming even as we gaze.

Sunrise, Sunset
Sunrise, Sunset
Swiftly fly the years.
One season following another
Laden with happiness and tears."

The Donut Tree

My wife has an annual wiener roast and hayride for her first grade Sunday School class. When we started the hayrides, we used hay wagons, tractors and trucks, later we rented a team of horses for a horse-drawn hayride. We often see flocks of grackles and geese migrating while on the ride. There is a covered bridge not far from our home, and we take the children to the covered bridge and have them get off the wagon and run through the dark covered bridge to the other side where we let them back on the wagon. Sometimes local farmers hide in the ditches along our route and jump out and scare us.

Back at the bonfire, there are always walks through the woods and a hunt for a bag of candy, but one of the children's favorite activities is the visit to the Donut Tree. The Donut Tree is an apple tree with powdered donuts hanging from strings. The children hold their hands behind their backs and the first one to eat the donut on the string wins. All of the children are covered with white powder after this game. The apple tree was severely damaged in a summer storm this year and will be cut down before our next party. Another tree will have to take over the responsibility of being the Donut Tree. The original Donut Tree will become part of the wood to feed the bonfire. For everything there is a season and a purpose.

Roasting hot dogs and marshmallows on an open fire is a first time experience for many of the children. There are usually more black hotdogs with ashes on them than expertly roasted hotdogs on a stick, but the children don't seem to mind. Trying to keep them from accidentally poking each other with the sticks is always a challenge.

When the children leave, they smell like smoke and they have straw on their clothes. They have smiles on their faces and white powder on their noses. The most important thing they leave with is a memory. A memory of a fun night outside under the stars when the air is crisp and the fire is warm. A memory of the taste of a roasted hotdog in a bun.

The day after the party, I start picking up sticks in the woods to build another brush pile to be used next year when the first graders come again to frolic on an October evening. They will do crafts, eat powdered donuts, play games, roast wieners and marshmallows, ride in a straw-filled, wooden wagon behind big, beautiful horses and watch flocks of birds fly south.

We moved into our old farmhouse at Middleton Corner in 1971. The house was built in 1891. It has been remodeled three times since we purchased it with additions in 1976 and then again in 2000. Consequently, our house was built in three centuries: 1800, 1900 and 2000.

My son, Kevin, grew up here. He spent time in the woods (it was a field then) making grass huts. That should have been an indication to me that he would go to college and study architecture. He did, and he now owns his own business in Ft. Myers, Florida, where he designs and builds homes and other structures. He designed the additions and changes to the original house that you see above.

During all the remodeling with the tearing out of walls, ceilings and floors, I always fantasized about finding hidden treasures somewhere. When the house was built in the 1800's, people in the country tended to not trust banks and they kept money hidden somewhere in the house or buried in a can in the yard or around the barn. The house was standing during the Great Depression when people hoarded their valuables. I think about digging up a can of money when I dig holes to plant bushes and trees in the garden. I would like to tell you that my fantasies became a reality and that I found jars of old coins worth lots of money, but I never found anything.

We have never torn out the ceiling, walls and floor of the basement to remodel so hope is still alive.

Daffodil Hill

Daffodil Hill is a project that took about ten years to complete and it was accomplished one bulb at a time with no cost to me. All I had invested was my labor. The old house we purchased at Middleton Corner in 1971 had two kinds of early yellow blooming daffodils planted around the foundation of the house. One variety was the single trumpet daffodil and the other was a double frilly variety. I did not particularly like the old fashioned flowers preferring the larger variety with more colors so I moved the daffodils to the field behind our house. About the same time my family started planting trees in the field because we wanted a woods. Eventually we had completely planted the field with trees and during the time the children were growing up, it grew into a young woods itself. It's been over thirty years now since the woods was planted and it is thick and full. During this time I dug and divided the daffodils in the woods and kept replanting them until eventually the whole two and one half acre woods was filled with yellow blooms each spring. Many people think you cannot plant daffodils in the springtime but this is not true. Daffodils can be transplanted just like any other garden plant. The advantage of dividing and replanting in the spring is that you can tell where all the other bulbs are planted. If you wait until fall, it becomes a guessing game as to where additional blooms are needed.

Because the old fashioned variety I used blooms much earlier than the cultivated bulbs in most modern gardens, there is a three-week display of color in early spring when it is needed most. This was one of the first things I did that brought attention to Middleton Corner and even John Middleton gave me credit for that!

People often come to photograph their children in the daffodils.

Straya

My daughter Karen was fond of cats and kittens when she was growing up at Middleton Corner. The only problem with this was that our house was real close to Highway U.S. 68 and cats didn't live very long even if they claimed all nine lives they are purported to have. Cars and trucks were unforgiving of a cat trying to cross from one side of the road to another.

I did not share my daughter's love of cats because they were daily digging holes in my flowerbeds and depositing their dung. I viewed them as daily dung diggers. Although I am an organic gardener who shuns commercial fertilizer in favor of natural animal by-products such as cow and horse manure, cat manure is too strong and lethal to ornamental plants.

When the last of Karen's cats was killed on the highway, I told her that she could not have any more cats. Most daughters have their fathers wrapped around their little fingers and I was no exception. When she pleaded with me with those beautiful eyes, I agreed that if a stray cat showed up that I would let her keep it.

The very next day, a pregnant calico cat showed up on our doorstep. Of course, I kept my word and allowed her to keep the cat. I wasn't too worried because I knew the cat would probably die on the highway anyway. However, to my surprise, the cat named Straya by my daughter, lived with us until Karen grew up and went away to college. Not only that, Straya was a prolific breeder. I have no idea how many kittens she produced. Karen confessed to me that she prayed that a stray cat would show up at our house. How can a father win when his daughter and God conspire against him? To my knowledge Straya never did die; one day she just disappeared. Two years later she reappeared and then disappeared for a final time. Maybe we should have called her Elija. He was taken to Heaven in a whirlwind and never died. The picture above is of Straya and my grandson, Alex.

Summer Sounds

We had chickens at Middleton Corner when the children were growing up. One of my favorite summer memories when I was in grade school was the sound of a hen clucking in the summer heat. I can't really describe the sound. It is something you have to hear. In fact, it was more than the sound, it was a total experience of the heat of the day, a warm breeze, bright sunshine, a clear blue sky, chickens sunning themselves in the dust, the smell of new mown hay, and hens making that clucking sound. These were carefree days when school was out and I wasn't old enough to hold a full time summer job or help with the hay baling. I had time to just experience the laziness of a hot summer day. I didn't know it then, but I was soaking up memories. Now when I hear a chicken clucking on a hot summer day, I immediately feel euphoric because it reminds me of those carefree days.

Another sound that makes me feel euphoric is to come home after dark on a summer evening and sit in the patio room with the doors open listening to the night sounds. There is a cacophony of ringing, chirping, clicking and croaking. It is hard to imagine how many crickets, how many katydids, how many cicadas and how many frogs it takes to create the night symphony. Every summer it sounds the same but it never grows old. It's a sound of summer nights that makes me happy.

The green cicada is one of my favorite ringing critters. They look like a huge horsefly, but unlike the horsefly they do not bite. One of the things I like to teach my grandsons is how much fun cicadas can be if you can find them and catch them. On a hot summer day you can hear the cicadas and think you know what direction the sound is coming from, but they are difficult to find even though they are often literally right under your nose. When I catch one, I hold it between my fingers and the cicada always starts to make its ringing noise. In doing so, it vibrates and tickles my fingers. I try to get the children to be brave enough to hold the cicada between their fingers so they can feel the vibration. When that happens and they feel the vibrations, they inevitably let the cicada go and it flies away to their sounds of glee.

Even with all the beauty and solitude at Middleton Corner, it can get boring at times. There are two highlights to every day Monday through Saturday, and that is the arrival of the mail and the delivery of the newspaper. Gerald Shaw is our rural mail carrier. He travels several miles up and down country roads but there is nothing peaceful about his trip down Highway U.S. 68. The traffic is usually heavy and the drivers are going fast. There are lots of semi trucks on this highway because R&L Transport is only four miles down the road at the junction with Interstate 71. Semis going fifty-five miles an hour cannot stop on a dime. There isn't much room to pull off the highway for Gerald to make his deliveries. A flashing yellow light on top of his vehicle and a sign on the back warning those behind him that he makes frequent stops are the only protection he has. One of the things that I am grateful for is that I do not have to cross the highway to get to my mailbox. One of my neighbors, Mr. Brickey, was hit while crossing the road to get his mail. Fortunately, he wasn't seriously injured.

Gerald is friendly and always puts our packages that are too big for the mailbox inside the door of the patio room. One day he accidentally locked his keys in his truck. He had to ask his wife to come from Cedarville with an additional key. While he waited for her arrival, he enjoyed the warmth of our home and a cup of coffee. We chatted about neighborhood issues. He is a gardener like me and when our paths cross and he is dropping off a package we talk about gardening. I shared some of my red cannas with him one year when he admired the six-foot tropical looking plants growing in the flowerbed beside the garage inside the back fence.

Miniature Hummingbird Returns to Middleton Corner

Hummingbirds are common in the area. However, it is always exciting to see these little wonders as they flit around sugar water feeders set up in the garden. I have a six-feeder station set up in a flowerbed by the garage so I can watch the hummers from the kitchen window. There are currently four hummingbirds that feed there regularly. By the end of the season last year, I had twelve hummers feeding and doing battle with each other. They are very territorial especially the males. When they do battle, it looks like fighter-bombers engaging in a dogfight in the sky.

Recently, I noticed what appeared to be a miniature hummingbird feeding on the purple phlox and pink lithrum in the garden. Every year about this time, these tiny hummingbird imposters appear. These hovering curiosities are actually day-flying moths known as hummingbird moths. Hummingbird clearwing moth is the species pictured. With a wingspan of two inches, the moth hovers while sipping nectar with a long "tongue," or proboscis just like a hummingbird. The hummingbird moth is a member of the family Hemaris Sphingidae, the same family as tomato hornworms. The larvae have curved tail "horns" and feed on honeysuckle. A slightly smaller relative closely resembles bumblebees. Anyone unfamiliar with the hummingbird moth can actually believe they have seen a miniature hummingbird.

The Barn

The barn was old when we moved to Middleton Corner. Termites had been feasting on it for some time. The roof had wooden shingles that had become brittle. It was impossible to walk on the roof without putting a hole in it. The barn roof sloped on the north side making it easy for a pet goat that our children owned to jump on the roof. Everywhere he stepped, he put a hole in the roof. For this reason, I had the kids put the goat on a chain and stake him out to graze. This worked great until one night during a violent thunderstorm he was struck by lightning and killed. I wasn't too upset about this but the kids loved the goat so we had a proper burial. I buried him with the chain still around his neck and planted an ash tree on his grave. The goat's name was Reuben so the ash tree became known to the family as the Reuben Tree. The incident has prompted two of my grandsons to write a short story called, "The Rattling Chain", about a goat ghost. He drags a chain around behind him. Every time you hear the sound of a rattling chain when the wind blows, something good happens the next day in the story.

The house we bought was built in 1891 so I have to assume that the barn was at least that old as well. I insured the barn along with the house hoping that a strong wind would blow the barn down and I could collect the insurance and put up a new barn. This never happened. In fact, on April 3, 1974, one of the largest tornadoes in recorded history destroyed most of Xenia, the nearest town to our home. I was chaperoning an after school dance in the gymnasium at Ankeney Junior High School in Beavercreek at the time the tornado hit. This is one of the worst possible locations to be in a school if hit by a tornado. I remember standing in the doorway watching the rain and hail. I love storms so this was a treat until we received a call that a tornado touched down in nearby Kettering. It jumped over the school and came back down on the city of Xenia, Ohio. On the way home I took the bypass around Xenia and could see nothing but destruction in all directions. I was sure my family was dead so you can imagine the feeling of relief I had when I came home to find no damage to the house or barn and when my wife and two small children emerged safely from the basement to greet me. The kids saw me cry for the first time.

The next day, I checked the barn and not one shingle had even been blown off the barn in this violent storm. Eventually a friend tore down the barn for the lumber. Wooden oak beams and pegs were worth something but I didn't know it. There were also large walnut boards covered with chicken poop.

John and Mona Faye Middleton

John and Mona Faye Middleton are the last of the clan still living at Middleton Corner. Even they flee to Naples, Florida, after John's birthday in January, and they don't return until April. John has declared himself the unofficial mayor. I assume that duty when he goes south for the winter. John and Mona Faye are great neighbors. My wife and I moved into an old farmhouse in 1971 that originally belonged to a Middleton. John has often quipped to me that it is up to me to put Middleton Corner on the map. I have tried to do that through a series of published news articles where I weave in the fact that the event is connected to Middleton Corner. Maybe with the publication of this book, John will finally leave me alone.

When I told him I would like to dedicate the book to him and his wife, he agreed only if I would mention his son, John, Jr., who passed away in 1973, a few days short of his 17th birthday. Johnny and his girlfriend, Karin Erd, were missing from Saturday evening until Sunday morning. One rumor was that they had run away to get married. Unfortunately, that was not true. Mona Faye discovered the bodies of the young couple in a parked car on Mother's Day. The two had parked on a secluded country road not far from Middleton Corner. They were overcome by carbon monoxide poisoning as they sat in the car. Mother's Day was forever changed for Mona Faye.

The Beach

Middleton Corner has a hidden beach and a swimming hole if you know where to look for it. When my kids were growing up in the seventies I was "a man of means by no means." Finances were tight with a young family and one income so we had to find fun things to do that didn't cost any money. One of our discoveries was Anderson Creek located on Engle Mill Road just off Spring-Valley Paintersville Road. This was only a short distance from our home.

A large accumulation of clean, soft sand had settled in a bend in the creek creating a natural "beach" where the kids could build sand castles. The water was somewhat clear and not very deep, so it was relatively safe if you didn't mind a water snake or two, some turtles, fish, toads and frogs as companions. My kids didn't mind. Fortunately, they didn't realize that many of their friends went to swimming pools with crystal clear water and no critters to contend with.

Sometimes on a sunny Sunday afternoon we would pack a lunch and have a picnic at our secret "beach." We never did see any other swimmers or creek enthusiasts on our visits, although I am sure we weren't the only locals to know of its existence.

I know my kids liked going there because when they had friends visit, they liked to take them to the "beach." The boys would fish, swim, catch toads and torment the girls.

My daughter, Karen, is now grown and the mother of two boys. She allows me to take my young grandsons to explore at the creek, but not to swim because like all things, the creek has changed and it is not as clean as it was when she built sand castles on the "beach."

Backyard Fence

Gary and Connie Downey are our neighbors over the backyard fence. Gary does construction work for a living and he almost totally remodeled the interior of our house during the time we have been neighbors. He would moonlight in the evenings and on weekends until the job was done. He did excellent work and always gave me a cheaper rate than other contractors.

He is the one who told me that the hippies we had rented to before we moved in had run around the house naked. There were no shades or curtains on the windows. He is the one who called me when the hippies beat their dog with a dead chicken because the dog had killed the chicken. Gary has a soft heart for animals and you don't hurt any of his dogs.

Gary has made pets out of two snapping turtles in the common ditch behind our houses. He feeds them scraps from his table and encourages me to do the same.

When we go on vacation, Gary watches our property, waters the plants and brings in the mail. Once we got stranded at the Atlantic Airport for four days because of an ice storm and Gary broke into our house to feed the dog when we called and told him our predicament.

The Downeys became adoptive parents with us. They adopted Kelly and Johnny and we adopted Michael. We now share pictures and stories about our grandchildren. Connie and Gary are pictured at the wedding of one of the boys they adopted. The backyard fence divides our property but it is the backyard fence that brought us together as friends.

Vacation Wonderland

People have described our place as like a park. We have a woods with walking trails, a small vernal stream with frogs, wildflowers, birds, chipmunks, squirrels, rabbits and a variety of other wildlife that inhabit the premises. We try to grow plants in the yard that attract butterflies, so in the summer it's like being outside among flying flowers. The same flowers also attract hummingbirds. One can sit in the patio room for hours watching their aerial antics. If you like to take pictures of nature, it's the place to be. In a previous entry I told you about the milkweed jungle growing in the yard that is nurtured because milkweeds are host plants for a variety of beautiful Ohio butterflies. My grandson, Tayler, is fascinated by the caterpillars he finds on the milkweeds that tower over his head. On this particular afternoon he found at least a dozen caterpillars grazing on the leaves. A chewed up milkweed plant is a good thing but it's not very pretty in the garden. The tradeoff is the sweet fragrance of the pink blooms in the spring, the "fairy" seeds that float in the air in the fall, and, of course, the plethora of butterflies that live in the yard because they can complete their life cycles there.

This is a great place for grandchildren to visit and a great place for Grandpa to teach them about nature.

What is it that makes a place special? Sights, sounds, and smells. We all remember coming home to the smell of Mom's home-baked cookies or popcorn. Smells can make us happy and become so much a part of us that we don't even think about them.

Middleton Corner has its own set of unique fragrances. There is a heavenly scent of the wafting fragrance of lilac on a spring breeze. There is the smell of the soil being turned in preparation for planting. Every kid knows the smell of fishing worms after a heavy summer rain. It signals a time to grab a bucket cause the worms are "easy pickins" and the fish are hungry!

Of course, not all smells are pleasant. A country resident soon learns to recognize when local farmers are cleaning their barns. Pig manure and cow manure have two very distinct odors and if I have to choose, I will choose cow manure over pig manure anytime! Sometime around February when there are occasional warm and sunny days, the skunks come out to prowl. All it takes is one impact with a car and the smell of the road kill permeates the air for days. However, since this is a harbinger of spring, even that smell is not too bad!

Nothing, but nothing beats the smell of new mown hay! The picture above was taken at the corner of Waynesville-Jamestown Road and St. John Road on a late August afternoon. It was the second cutting of hay for the season. Farmers now bale hay alone without the aid of teenage boys to load the wagons. Gone are the days of sweating and building muscles from lifting fifty pound bales and stacking them over your head on a moving wagon.

This vignette is a tribute to my wife, Norma. She has proofed every page in this book for me, but she won't see this page until after the book is published. She is one of the most humble and kind people that I know. She would not want me to focus the reader's attention on her. I realized shortly after we were married that Norma was a "born teacher." Truly great teachers, I believe are innately wired to teach and are not really trained by a university or mentor program. I am not putting these programs down because they do help the born teacher hone her skills and increase her bag of tricks, but they don't make her a teacher. When we were married, Norma was working as an executive secretary with a two-year associates degree. Shortly after our marriage, we took over a cottage of fifteen pre-teen boys at the Ohio Soldiers and Sailor's Orphan's Home. Norma did amazing things in teaching the boys. This lasted a year until she became pregnant with our oldest son and we left that position. She was an excellent mother and did all the right things to teach our children even before they were born. Our next joint venture was when I became superintendent of the Greene County Children's Home and she assumed the role of matron planning meals, purchasing clothes and planning recreational activities for the children. A second pregnancy and the closing of the children's home led us to a Girls' Group Home which lasted a short time because the troubled teenagers threatened physical harm to our children. After this she watched a whole house full of children while their parents worked. She was always doing something to help with the family income. While doing all this, she took college classes at Central State University and graduated with a four-year degree in elementary education. By this time our children were ready to start school and she began substitute teaching until she secured a job at Arrowood Elementary School in Xenia, Ohio. She has been in the same school and the same room for twenty-seven years. She has taught over six hundred children to read! The amazing thing about her twenty-seven years of teaching is that she was diagnosed with Crohn's Disease during her third year of teaching. Three years ago on the second day of school she slipped on water in the hallway at school and ruptured a disk in her back. Physical therapy and surgery have not taken away the pain and yet she continues to teach without complaining. She describes teaching as her mission. Her teaching motto is, "Love them into learning." She is an inspiration to me and to everyone who knows her. Her students love her and so do I.

Wallace D. Campbell was born in 1944 in Clarksville, Ohio, to Ralph and Armetha Campbell. He has two sisters - Ella Kay and Wanda, and six brothers – Albert Benny, James, Glenn, Keith, Kent, and Richard. His parents and brother, Glenn, are deceased.

He worked as a playground supervisor and relief houseparent at The Ohio Soldiers and Sailors Orphans Home while attending college. He was the superintendent of the Greene County Children's Home, and he worked in a girls' group home. He taught high school special education, an Occupational Work Adjustment class at Beavercreek High School and 8th grade math and science at Ferguson Junior High School. He served as a junior high assistant principal and principal at Ankeney Junior High School in Beavercreek. He worked for several years as the Curriculum Director K-12 for West Carrollton City Schools. He retired from public education in 1995 with thirty-one years experience. He began working the next Monday as Manager of Education and Training for the Greene County Mental Retardation and Developmentally Delayed (MRDD) Board. He was briefly assigned to the MRDD Early Intervention Center. After that he became the assistant principal at Greeneview High School where he is currently the principal. He was named the Ohio Assistant Principal of the Year while at Greeneview. He earned both a bachelor's and master's degree in education at Central State University. He also graduated from the University of Dayton with an Educational Specialist degree and a doctorate in Educational Leadership. After graduating from college the first time, he met and married his wife of thirty-nine years, Norma Coy. Together they raised four children, a foster son, an adopted son and a son and daughter born of their union. Their children - Kenny, Kevin, Michael and Karen are all grown and have families of their own. He has five grandchildren: Alex, Tayler, Tanner, Jacob, and Isaac. He is an avid gardener who loves photography and writing. He tries to focus his readers on the beauty of God in all of creation through his writing, photography and gardening. He hopes to have planted a tree on the day he enters Heaven to worship the Awesome Creator who allowed him the privilege of enjoying His creations.

Caterpillar munching on milkweed leaf at Middleton Corner

Goldenrod flourishes at Middleton Corner. Butterflies love the sweet nectar of the blooms.

Printed in the United States
by Baker & Taylor Publisher Services